THE FAIR DEAL:

I0422542

A Plan To Cancel The

National Debt & Restore

Fiscal Accountability!

by

Dennis Andrew Ball,

author, THE BALL DOCTRINE:

"Creating Peace & Prosperity In Every Nation!"

ISBN 13: 9781544659909
10: 1544659903

DEDICATION

"THIS BOOK IS DEDICATED TO AMERICANS

WHO SACRIFICE EVERYDAY TO PRESERVE

PROTECT & DEFEND OUR LIBERTY &

FREEDOM FOR OUR CHILDREN&

GENERATIONS TO COME!

NOW THE TIME HAS COME FOR A NEW

GENERATION OF AMERICANS TO TAKE THE

REIGNS OF STATE & MAKE THEM WORK AS

THEIR OWN IN THE BEST INTERSTS OF THE

PEOPLE, THEIR CHILDREN, THEIR FAMILIES

AND GENERATIONS TO COME!

TABLE OF CONTENTS

Dedication

Acknowledgment

Authors' Foreword

———

ACKNOWLEDGMENT

To The COURAGE President Franklin D. Roosevelt Demonstrated At A Time Of Great Danger To Our Nation During Uncertain Times In American History.

Author's Foreword

I am reminded by history past the history of the United States would not be complete if it were not for those gallant men and women who in the face of danger, proceeded to do something Special about it! America's very existence is tied to her economic health which has seen a great deal of danger for THE PEOPLE since 1913 starting at Jekyl Island, Georgia by a group of elitist Domestic & International bankers with the participation of the Congress of the United States on Christmas Eve. This is the premise for **THE FAIR DEAL: "A Plan To Cancel The National Debt & Restore Fiscal Accountability!"**

5

Since the death of President Kennedy, events in America and the World have continued to show all of us how vulnerable our economic system is to currency manipulation and deficit spending by governments and the Congress of these United States, the result being a bloated deficit with borrowing and spending unaccountable to The Citizenry & States of the United States; including fiscal policies, laws and acts contrary to The BEST INTERESTS of ALL Americans.

THE FAIR DEAL addresses these abuses showing the way out of the fiscal crisis generations of government entities have allowed to be created including every President since President Kennedy.

*Now the magic of **Real Change** can come through THE FAIR DEAL: "A Plan To Cancel The National Debt & Restore Fiscal Accountability". Read what must done to solve the fiscal crisis in America and the World.*

6

1. *THE FAIR DEAL!*

The *history of America* would not be complete if it were not for the men and women
who sacrificed so much of themselves for a new nation and its children. Of course, much can be said of those who plotted against them and used them to profit at their expense. For those they must answer for us we must correct their mistakes for our children and generations to come. This then, becomes the back ground and back drop of *THE FAIR DEAL!*

"You cannot help the poor by destroying the Rich." "You cannot keep out of trouble by spending more than you earn." "You cannot lift the wage earner by pulling down the wage payer" – Abraham Lincoln

---

"I have always been afraid of banks."

7

"One man with courage makes a majority"
"It is to be regretted that the rich and powerful

too often bend the acts of government to their own selfish purposes." "Take time to deliberate but when the time for action arrives,

stop thinking and go in." – *Andrew Jackson*

Let it be said, that America's finest hours are yet to come because the Children Of America can make a contribution to not only our Nation but also the World!

We are the product of generations past, present and future with the belief that our rights come from God; NOT THE STATE at a great cost to those who fought and died for them! That was the Social Contract created in 1781 at Yorktown-Gloucester Bay, Virginia.

The monuments laid at the reefs of those so honored are a testament to the sacrifice of so many for the hope that their sacrifice would *bear*. A proud nation was born and with it the greatest nation on earth in the history of man, "*AMERICA!*"

THE NATIONAL BACKGROUND
Early History

What was assumed by those in power was taken for granted by those struggling to live out their dreams. *AMERICA* was a land of opportunity because it's people made it their priority to continue living out their dreams for a better life for themselves and those for their children.

Colonial America grew at an astounding rate by the span of time from the founding of the Republic at Jamestown, Virginia 1607 until the last entry known as Georgia Colony 1732.

Of course, many events in between the time of founding and establishing Colonial life dominated the culture legally and politically;

9

particularly making it possible for 2.5 million people to realize their value because the Bible was read in the home, the schools and the Supreme Court! Ethics & Morales were also taught in the home practicing honesty and good business including honest services. The attitudes within the culture was fairness as the colonies grew in population and farming. As a result, the *Great Migration* ensued so that by the beginning of the War For Independence, *AMERICA* had enough population to fight England for it. And so we did on July 4, 1776 by way of the Declaration Of Independence, Congress, Philadelphia, Pennsylvania.

Now comes THE FAIR DEAL redefining the current rules based on the *16th Amendment to the Constitution of these United States.* What does it say and what does it mean?

"*CONGRESS,* shall have power to lay & collect taxes on incomes without

10

regard to any census or enumeration. There was an income tax *prior* to this Amendment & it was in effect during the Civil War." Ratified February 3, 1913

So, what we have here is a system of taxation based on representation of enumeration of census as to the number of folks occupy individual states. However, this Amendment did away with the census enumeration and went to a direct tax on income which now includes the Standard Deduction and deductions based on losses and gains. Could it be those with the most to lose tie themselves up with the government for as long as necessary to keep themselves from being penalized for surreptitious acts they commit during the period of doing their business?

That is my point, unlike the history of *Early America* when life and government was

11

much simpler and much smaller than now, we Americans did not have to deal with so much regulation and taxation without representation. Executive session was the oddity not common experience as is *today.*

And So, since President William Howard Taft, a man who held Office as both President and later as Chief Justice, history records his participation in the events that mark 1913 as a Turning point in American history.

Events do have a way of marking themselves to follow the outcome of what creates tremendous conflicts and tragedy in the lives of our Citizens and the outcome for our Children.

It is within this context that government *Of, By & For The People* will survive and thrive in this the twenty-first century and beyond.

THE FAIR DEAL is that vehicle to get there and make every other model obsolete in the process.

12

So WHAT are we talking about and HOW do we get there?

2. THE FEDERAL RESERVE ACT

DECEMBER 24, 1913 SIXTEEN PAGES PRICE TWO CENTS

PRESIDENT'S SIGNATURE ENACTS CURRENCY LAW

Wilson Declares It the First of Series of Constructive Acts to Aid Business.

Makes Speech to Group of Democratic Leaders.

Conference Report Adopted in Senate by Vote of 43 to 25.

Banks All Over the Country Hasten to Enter Federal Reserve System.

Gov-Elect Walsh Calls Passage of Bill A Fine Christmas Present.

WILSON SEES DAWN OF NEW ERA IN BUSINESS

Aims to Make Prosperity Free to Have Unimpeded Momentum.

HOME VIEWS OF CURRENCY ACT

FOUR PENS USED BY PRESIDENT

This is the man that betrayed America and made us into a debtor nation! Woodrow Wilson, President Of The United States! Signed into law December 23, 1913. He was A

also the President that led the United States into World War 1 at the behest of the International Banking Cartel who financed both World Wars and have ever since! How convenient!

This is what Presidents' Washington, Lincoln and Jackson warned Americans not to let government become BIG Government at the expense of the Common man. They knew our economic health depended upon the strength of a strong dollar able to compete in the Global Marketplace unimpeded by fraud and schemes.

In Europe, the same holds true especially in the United Kingdom. Both The House Of Lords & The House Of Commons take their

14

marching orders from the Queen of England closely administered by the Central Bank Of England.

That is how the International Monetary Fund & World Bank became the Central Banks of Europe by following policy from the Crown. All the other countries followed its lead and created what today is the European Union which ironically recently the UK withdrew by a vote of the people. To many Brits, especially the Ruling Class, the EU has become an albatross around their necks by it's economic and political interests.

The Federal Reserve Act of 1913 set the stage for economic chaos not only for America but the entire World! Manipulation of currency laws in every country based on Central Bank policy has put the Bankers in control of the World; not THE PEOPLE!

There is a complete disconnect between what is *fair* and what is *just!* By making nations

15

debtors to the Banks, the children & families suffer for lack of "equitable advantage". Laws that govern borrowing and spending create debt by which those in control benefit handsomely at the debtors expense which in many cases are families. More will be written about this subject as I lay out a plan to restore the family both economically and emotionally in their BEST INTERESTS for generations to come.

The Act cemented in the minds of many the desire for Banks to create Central Banks to administer the flow of currency and capital to their members. But again, the price was a Surrender of economic sovereignty to the banks which is the root of the problem in the World. "He that controls the Gold controls the Nation State", said Lord Cromwell. The *history* of the corruption does not stop there.

1913 was an interesting year for America not only for the signing by President Wilson but the ratification of the 16th Amendment by The State Of Wyoming providing ¾ majority of states necessary to amend the Constitution. The first IRS 1040 also rolled out to finance Wars as it continues TODAY. *(See exhibits)*

TO BE FILLED IN BY COLLECTOR.	Form 1040.	TO BE FILLED IN BY INTERNAL REVENUE BUREAU.

INCOME TAX.

List. No. ....

.... District of ....

Date received ....

THE PENALTY
FOR FAILURE TO HAVE THIS RETURN IN
THE HANDS OF THE COLLECTOR OF
INTERNAL REVENUE ON OR BEFORE
MARCH 1 IS $20 TO $1,000.
(SEE INSTRUCTIONS ON PAGE 4.)

File No. ....

Assessment List ....

Page .... Line ....

UNITED STATES INTERNAL REVENUE.

RETURN OF ANNUAL NET INCOME OF INDIVIDUALS.
(As provided by Act of Congress, approved October 3, 1913.)

RETURN OF NET INCOME RECEIVED OR ACCRUED DURING THE YEAR ENDED DECEMBER 31, 191 ....
(FOR THE YEAR 1913, FROM MARCH 1, TO DECEMBER 31.)

Filed by (or for) .... of ....
(Full name of individual.) (Street and No.)

in the City, Town, or Post Office of .... State of ....
(Fill in pages 2 and 3 before making entries below.)

1. GROSS INCOME (see page 2, line 12)	$	
2. GENERAL DEDUCTIONS (see page 3, line 7)	$	
3. NET INCOME	$	

Deductions and exemptions allowed in computing income subject to the normal tax of 1 per cent.

4. Dividends and net earnings received or accrued, of corporations, etc., subject to like tax. (See page 2, line 11) . . .	$	
5. Amount of income on which the normal tax has been deducted and withheld at the source. (See page 2, line 9, column A)		
6. Specific exemption of $3,000 or $4,000, as the case may be. (See Instructions 3 and 19)		

Total deductions and exemptions. (Items 4, 5, and 6) . . . . $

7. TAXABLE INCOME on which the normal tax of 1 per cent is to be calculated. (See Instruction 3) . $

8. When the net income shown above on line 3 exceeds $20,000, the additional tax thereon must be calculated as per schedule below:

						INCOME.	TAX.
1	per cent on amount over $20,000 and not exceeding $50,000 . .					$	$
2	"	"	50,000	"	"	75,000 .		
3	"	"	75,000	"	"	100,000 .		
4	"	"	100,000	"	"	250,000 .		
5	"	"	250,000	"	"	500,000 .		
6	"	"	500,000	. . . .				

Total additional or super tax . . . . $

Total normal tax (1 per cent of amount entered on line 7) . . $

Total tax liability . . . . $

18

2

GROSS INCOME.

This statement must show in the proper spaces the entire amount of gains, profits, and income received by or accrued to the individual from all sources during the year specified on page 1.

DESCRIPTION OF INCOME.	A. Amount of income on which tax has been deducted and withheld at the source.	B. Amount of income on which tax has NOT been deducted and withheld at the source.
1. Total amount derived from salaries, wages, or compensation for personal service of whatever kind and in whatever form paid	$	$
2. Total amount derived from professions, vocations, businesses, trade, commerce, or sales or dealings in property, whether real or personal, growing out of the ownership or use of interest in real or personal property, including bonds, stocks, etc.		
3. Total amount derived from rents and from interest on notes, mortgages, and securities (other than reported on lines 5 and 6)		
4. Total amount of gains and profits derived from partnership business, whether the same be divided and distributed or not		
5. Total amount of fixed and determinable annual gains, profits, and income derived from interest upon bonds and mortgages or deeds of trust, or other similar obligations of corporations, joint-stock companies or associations, and insurance companies, whether payable annually or at shorter or longer periods		
6. Total amount of income derived from coupons, checks, or bills of exchange for or in payment of interest upon bonds issued in *foreign countries* and upon *foreign mortgages* or like obligations (not payable in the United States), and also from coupons, checks, or bills of exchange for or in payment of any dividends upon the stock or interest upon the obligations of foreign corporations, associations, and insurance companies engaged in business in foreign countries		
7. Total amount of income received from fiduciaries		
8. Total amount of income derived from any source whatever, not specified or entered elsewhere on this page		
9. TOTALS		
NOTES.—Enter total of Column A on line 5 of first page.		
10. AGGREGATE TOTALS OF COLUMNS A AND B	$	
11. Total amount of income derived from dividends on the stock or from the net earnings of corporations, joint-stock companies, associations, or insurance companies subject to like tax (To be entered on line 4 of first page.)	$	
12. TOTAL "Gross Income" (to be entered on line 1 of first page)	$	

19

3

GENERAL DEDUCTIONS.

1. The amount of necessary expenses actually paid in carrying on business, but not including business expenses of partnerships, and not including personal, living, or family expenses .	$			
2. All interest paid within the year on personal indebtedness of taxpayer				
3. All national, State, county, school, and municipal taxes paid within the year (not including those assessed against local benefits)				
4. Losses actually sustained during the year incurred in trade or arising from fires, storms, or shipwreck, and not compensated for by insurance or otherwise				
5. Debts due which have been actually ascertained to be worthless and which have been charged off within the year				
6. Amount representing a reasonable allowance for the exhaustion, wear, and tear of property arising out of its use or employment in the business, not to exceed, in the case of mines, 5 per cent of the gross value at the mine of the output for the year for which the computation is made, but no deduction shall be made for any amount of expense of restoring property or making good the exhaustion thereof, for which an allowance is or has been made . . .				
7. Total "General Deductions" (to be entered on line 2 of first page)				

AFFIDAVIT TO BE EXECUTED BY INDIVIDUAL MAKING HIS OWN RETURN.

I solemnly swear (or affirm) that the foregoing return, to the best of my knowledge and belief, contains a true and complete statement all gains, profits, and income received by or accrued to me during the year for which the return is made, and that I am entitled to all the deduct and exemptions entered or claimed therein, under the Federal Income-tax Law of October 3, 1913.

Sworn to and subscribed before me this ....

day of .... , 191   ....
                                                         (Signature of individual.)

SEAL OF OFFICER TAKING AFFIDAVIT.	....
	....
	(Official capacity.)

AFFIDAVIT TO BE EXECUTED BY DULY AUTHORIZED AGENT MAKING RETURN FOR INDIVIDUAL.

I solemnly swear (or affirm) that I have sufficient knowledge of the affairs and property of .... to enable me to make a full and complete return thereof, and that the foregoing return, to the best of my knowledge and belief, contains a and complete statement of all gains, profits, and income received by or accrued to said individual during the year for which the return is m and that the said individual is entitled, under the Federal Income-tax Law of October 3, 1913, to all the deductions and exemptions enter claimed therein.

Sworn to and subscribed before me this ....

day of .... , 191   ....
                                                         (Signature of agent.)

SEAL OF OFFICER TAKING AFFIDAVIT.	ADDRESS IN FULL { ....
....	....
(Official capacity.)	

[SEE INSTRUCTIONS ON BACK OF THIS PAGE.]

INSTRUCTIONS.

1. This return shall be made by every citizen of the United States, whether residing at home or abroad, and by every person residing in the United States, though not a citizen thereof, having a *net income* of $3,000 or over for the taxable year, and *also* by every *nonresident alien* deriving income from property owned and business, trade, or profession carried on *in the United States* by him.

2. When an individual by reason of minority, sickness or other disability, or absence from the United States, is unable to make his own return, it may be made for him by his *duly authorized* representative.

3. The *normal tax* of 1 per cent shall be assessed on the total net income less the specific exemption of $3,000 or $4,000 as the case may be. (For the year 1913, the specific exemption allowable is $2,500 or $3,333.33, as the case may be.) If, however, the normal tax has been deducted and withheld on any part of the income at the source, or if any part of the income is received as dividends upon the stock or from the net earnings of any corporation, etc., which is taxable upon its net income, such income shall be deducted from the individual's *total net income* for the purpose of calculating the amount of income on which the individual is liable for the normal tax of 1 per cent by virtue of this return. (See page 1, line 7.)

4. The *additional or super tax* shall be calculated as stated on page 1.

5. This return shall be filed with the Collector of Internal Revenue for the district in which the individual resides if he has no other place of business, otherwise in the district in which he has his *principal place of business;* or in case the person resides in a foreign country, then with the collector for the district in which his principal business is carried on in the United States.

6. This return must be filed on or before the first day of March succeeding the close of the calendar year for which return is made.

7. The *penalty for failure to file the return within the time specified by law* is $20 to $1,000. In case of refusal or neglect to render the return within the required time (except in cases of sickness or absence), 50 per cent shall be added to amount of tax assessed. In case of *false or fraudulent return*, 100 per cent shall be added to such tax, and any person required by law to make, render, sign, or verify any return who makes any false or fraudulent return or statement with intent to defeat or evade the assessment required by this section to be made shall be guilty of a misdemeanor, and shall be fined not exceeding $2,000 or be imprisoned not exceeding one year, or both, at the discretion of the court, with the costs of prosecution.

8. When the return is not filed within the required time by reason of sickness or absence of the individual, an extension of time, not exceeding 30 days from March 1, within which to file such return, *may be* granted by the collector, *provided* an application therefor is made by the individual within the period for which such extension is desired.

9. This return properly filled out must be made under oath or affirmation. Affidavits may be made before any officer *authorized by law* to administer oaths. If before a justice of the peace or magistrate; not using a seal, a *certificate of the clerk of the court as to the authority* of such officer to administer oaths should be *attached to the return.*

10. Expense for medical attendance, store accounts, family supplies, wages of domestic servants, cost of board, room, or house rent for family or personal use, *are not expenses that can be deducted from gross income.* In case an individual owns his own residence he can not deduct the estimated value of his rent, neither shall he be required to include such estimated rental of his home as income.

11. The farmer, in computing the net income from his farm for his annual return, shall include all moneys received for produce and animals sold, and for the wool and hides of animals slaughtered, provided such wool and hides are sold, and he shall deduct therefrom the sums actually paid as purchase money for the animals sold or slaughtered during the year.

When animals were raised by the owner and are sold or slaughtered he shall not deduct their value as expenses or less. He may deduct the amount of money actually paid as expense for producing any farm products, live stock, etc. In deducting expenses for repairs on farm property the amount deducted must not exceed the amount actually expended for such repairs during the year for which the return is made. (See page 3, item 6.) The cost of replacing tools or machinery is a deductible expense to the extent that the cost of the new articles does not exceed the value of the old.

12. In calculating losses, only such losses as shall have been actually sustained and the amount of which has been definitely ascertained during the year covered by the return can be deducted.

13. Persons receiving fees or emoluments for professional or other services, as in the case of physicians or lawyers, should include all actual receipts for services rendered in the year for which return is made, together with all unpaid accounts, charges for services, or contingent income due for that year, if good and collectible.

14. Debts which were contracted during the year for which return is made, but found in said year to be worthless, may be deducted from gross income for said year, but such debts can not be regarded as worthless until after legal proceedings to recover the same have proved fruitless, or it clearly appears that the debtor is insolvent. If debts contracted prior to the year for which return is made were included as income in return for year in which said debts were contracted, and such debts shall subsequently prove to be worthless, they may be deducted under the head of losses in the return for the year in which such debts were charged off as worthless.

15. Amounts due or accrued to the individual members of a partnership from the net earnings of the partnership, whether apportioned and distributed or not, shall be included in the annual return of the individual.

16. United States pensions shall be included as income.

17. Estimated advance in value of real estate is not required to be reported as income, unless the increased value is taken up on the books of the individual as an increase of assets.

18. Costs of suits and other legal proceedings arising from ordinary business may be treated as an expense of such business, and may be deducted from gross income for the year in which such costs were paid.

19. An unmarried individual or a married individual not living with wife or husband shall be allowed an exemption of $3,000. When husband and wife live together they shall be allowed jointly a total exemption of only $4,000 on their aggregate income. They may make a joint return, both subscribing thereto, or if they have separate incomes, they may make separate returns; but in no case shall they jointly claim more than $4,000 exemption on their aggregate income.

20. In computing net income there shall be excluded the compensation of all officers and employees of a State or any political subdivision thereof, except when such compensation is paid by the United States Government.

The Banker's Cartel begins to roll since their secret meeting in 1910 on the Resort island known as Jekyl Island, GA.

3. PRESIDENT KENNEDY

"The High Office Of The President Has Been Used To Foment A Plot To Destroy The Americans' Freedom & Before I Leave Office I Must Inform The Citizens Of This Plight".

President John Fitzgerald Kennedy, Columbia University November. 12, 1963.

What the President alluded to was the pernicious attitude upon the nation by the Cartel of International Bankers President Woodrow Wilson had signed into law a day prior to Christmas Eve December 23, 1913.

The Federal Reserve Act was a continuation of the financial abuse created upon the nation prior to its signing, in 1791 & 1816. Only Old Hickory shut down the Bank Of The United States in 1836 paying off the Federal Debt of $7,000,000.00 with The Federal Treasury. It still stands today.

Because of what the Banking Cartel had

22

done to the nation, President Kennedy was intent in undoing. Because the Federal Reserve Bank is a Central Bank its Charter exempted it from accountable oversight to any government entity. Its powers had to be reigned in.

John Kennedy made it his business to do just that by signing E.O. 11110 effectively transferring control of the Bank out of their hands to the United States Treasury. This in turn had the chilling effect of neutralizing the Bank's Charter putting it out of business. The Gold Standard still was backing US Dollar currency for The People.

Signed June 4, 1963, the Order provided for the printing of both Silver Certificates & United States Notes exempting the words Federal Reserve Note. Both bills showed their authenticity to the United States Treasury and were circulated prior to and shortly after President Kennedy's death November 22, 1963. That Order has never been rescinded but ignored by every President since Kennedy. The National debt does not belong to the American People but to the private banking cartel known as the Federal Reserve Bank Of NY & its Branches!

***** *(for educational Art display only)*

RS - ($2.00 United States Note Circa 1963)

RS - ($5.00 United States Note Circa 1963)

***** *(for educational Art display only)*

4.   FAIR   TAX
ACT!H.R.25;S.18(2017)

Because the Fair Tax REPLACES the Income Tax, the Federal government is concerned about their money supporting a system that is bankrupt supporting a national debt with tax payer dollars. House Rules Committee Bill 25 aka The Fair Tax Act as Introduced by House Representative Rob Woodall, R-GA-7] 01/03/2017, 115th Congress.

Official Title:

AS introduced – To promote freedom, fairness, & economic opportunity by repealing The Income Tax & other taxes, abolishing the Internal Revenue Service; enacting a National Sales Tax to be administered primarily by the States.

Under the bill, the States have the responsibility for collecting & remitting the sales tax to the United States Treasury. Tax Revenues are to allocate amongst 5 groups. They are:

1. General Revenue Funds.

2. Old-age & Survivors Insurance Trust Fund.

3. Disability Insurance Trust Fund.

4. Hospital Insurance Trust Fund.

5. Federal Supplementary Medical Insurance Trust Fund.

NO FUNDING is authorized for the operations of Internal Revenue Service after Fiscal Year [FY2021].

The Bill terminates the national sales tax if the Sixteenth Amendment to the Constitution (authorizing an income tax) is not repealed within seven years after the enactment of this bill.

United States Senate Version:

S. 18 - Introduced Senator Jerry Moran, [R-KS] 1/3/2017. The Senate version is similar to that of the House but for a few additions and subtractions including a monthly sales tax rebate based on size of family and poverty guidelines. Both bills still have a lot of work to do upon which a Balance Budget Amendment to the Constitution is also necessary to keep government from overspending by bad policy that encourages it including a tax rate of 23% the first year which is much too high.

What is necessary is for the States to take back responsibility to tell the Federal Government how much money they are to fund essential services and DOD. The purpose of government is to protect its Citizens from threats to their lives, property money and Bill Of Rights; NOT TO GROW AN OUT OF CONTROL GOVERNMENT AT THE EXPENSE OF ITS CITIZENS.

5. BALANCED BUDGET!

The Federal Government is undisciplined by design the case for a balanced budget and with it a Balanced Budget Amendment.

The case can also be made that unfunded mandates it creates causes harm to the States by depleting their resources for the citizens in their State.

SOPHISTRY has literally changed the Mission & Purpose of Federal government to one of consumption & waste of Taxpayer dollars.

Entitlements, Earmarks, Pork, Mandates, Gerrymandering and getting re-elected with few term limits have caused a burgeoning national debt and crisis of confidence in our nation's economy.

28

How much more can the nation endure until real change addresses the real problems of Income Inequality? Only time will tell, but in this author's humble opinion, it needs to start NOW!

The budget of the United States has always been a hot button issue because of the demands of government on The People.

One can compare their own experience to everyday life of demands placed on our time and resources. So it is with problems created by government and an out-of-control undisciplined spending that causes harm to our nation and our lives.

To correct that requires more than wishful thinking. We must have a plan and make it a part of our national dialogue and life. "WE CAN!""WE WILL!" should be a slogan echoed in the Halls of Congress.

Our children will thank us for making it and them our priority to secure their futures and those to come.

Replacing the 16th Amendment with a Balance Budget Amendment makes sense. Bridling the Federal Budget from politicians who use their position to buy votes with tax payer dollars in the form of Pork, Earmarks Mandates, Entitlements, Sophistry is wrong!

How many school lunch programs for little kids are we depriving by masking our true intentions in ways that hurt our nation and our Children?

On the streets of Washington D.C. I witnessed in 2012 homeless people and families sleeping on the streets and sides of buildings for not enough food to ear or a place to sleep. In a country as rich as these United States, I saw what poverty does to people and the aftermath of hopelessness makes. Skilled Labor prevents that social experience of homelessness. Making life affordable is the challenge we face and it starts with the budget economy that works for all Americans and their families. From there, Citizenship becomes the responsibility of us all to see our children are educated and our community productive. Skilled labor solves a multitude of problems politicians create.

A Balanced Budget amendment will keep Federal departments from overspending and gaming the system for more resources the next fiscal year. With the States processing the tax on consumption, they will be in the

31

position to take control of the purse to empower them to control the size and depth of the Federal government because controls on spending and borrowing do not exist. It is within their discretion based on revenues collected at the State level to fund having the effect of limiting the size of government and its wasteful spending practices on non-essential services & programs based on the taxes in their control.

6. STATE REVENUE.DEPTS.

"The States Have The Responsibility For Administering, Collecting & Allocating The Sales Tax To The Treasury." – The Fair Tax

Because NO provision was written into The United States Constitution regulating Borrowing or spending by the Congress of these United States, there exists and has for years, a problem regulating the National Debt beginning in 1913 continuing until now.

That problem is DEFICIT SPENDING. borrowing and paying Interest on the Debt with taxpayer dollars out of the Federal Treasury. This is what George Washington warned America at its founding and to keep America "Free" from its burden as if foreign

33

Army's had absconded with government property without ever firing a shot!

In our history, the problem has grown to become UNACCOUNTABLE DEFICIT BORROWING & SPENDING making it IMPOSSIBLE for the Federal Government to police itself without shutting it down.;

Our history also shows that since 1913, *America* has failed to put in place safeguards to prevent this unaccountable cycle to come to an END!. WE THE PEOPLE, demand that this government stop it's endless cycle for the good of our Country, our Children and Generations to come!

The Ruling Banking Families in the Federal Reserve Central Bank know exactly the burden they have created by design upon the American people & their children. They know the bigger the debt on the nation the greater their profits from the DEFICIT. They are not about to reduce it because they know they don't have too. But that does not release them from the liability of their FRAUD on the nation. Specifically, Executive Order E.O 11110 signed June 4, 1963 by then President John Fitzgerald Kennedy transferring control of America's monetary system to the United States Treasury.

We can see that in June 1963, America Borrowed $305,859,632,996.41 backed by Gold & Silver.   Today, the debt has grown and keeps growing to unacceptable limits all to make the Bankers more money on interest charged on THEIR DEBT.

-Here's The Evidence-

From 1963 to 1999 The National debt climbed from $305,000,000,000.00 billions to over $5,000,000,000,000.00 trillions.in a matter of 36 years. Now it is approaching $20,000,000,000,000,.00 with trillions in Unfunded mandates stuck to the States.

The Cartel has made its business to loan the Federal Government any amount of *fiat* currency it requires as long as it pays the interest on the debt. They have also made it their business to cause harm to Citizens by causing the government to collect taxes to pay them. The debt however, cannot be paid *but it can be forgiven.*

How? Because it is backed by nothing! The same people who formed the Cartel sold the Country that the Banks would take care of the financial needs of the nation so long as the nation paid them interest on the debt. The Federal Reserve System is neither Federal nor a Reserve of Currency nor a System. It is in effect a Banker's Cartel who lends *fiat currency with no value for interest payments to the members of the Cartel every month administered by the IRS & Treasury.*

This relationship was designed by the Scientists of the Federal Reserve System. They knew exactly what they should do to make the "System" work for them opposite the American Taxpayer.

In effect, it is a corrupt institution that Funds the International Monetary Fund & The World Bank.

There is absolutely no evidence that

Executive Order 11110 signed June 4, 1963 has been rescinded or the wording that nullified it despite other President's issues.

We are left that since every President since Lyndon Johnson, has ignored it that perhaps fearful that if they were to follow its directive, they too might be killed. Both Lincoln and Kennedy believed the *Nation* Should issue and regulate its own currency, not a foreign bank masquerading around as a Federal entity but a private banking cartel.

The nation had seen this before during the presidency of Andrew Jackson (1829-1837).

THE BANK OF THE UNITED STATES was shut down by Jackson but an attempt was made on his life. Jackson, founder of the Democratic Party surmised as warned by

George Washington that the currency of the nation was sovereign to the United States Treasury and should stay in its control both in the manufacturing and minting of printed and coined currency.

The inflation non-backed currency wars on the dollar devaluing the dollars' worth in terms of purchasing power and payment of debt release. Diluting the economy with unbacked green backs is a recipe for more inflation and higher prices.

Backed securities with Gold or Silver makes for a much more stable economy disallowing the government from over spending and causing families harm by a reckless and selfish policy of greed.

THE FAIR DEAL will cause the Federal government to shrink because it will no longer be able to control a rogue policy of self enrichment at the expense of the taxpayers and their families. The Federal government will have to learn to live within its means like Citizens must live within a budget. The Charter Bank will replace the Central Bank aka Federal Reserve System.

The boom and bust cycles in the *history* of the nation is over. Economic prosperity for America will be measured in real dollars backed by Gold or Silver instead of nothing!

The national debt will be gone and the dawning of a new era in funding will begin! War bonds, Saving Bonds, Treasury Bills all have their place raising money for worthy Causes and Investments for the The People!

7.REPEAL16THAMENDMENT

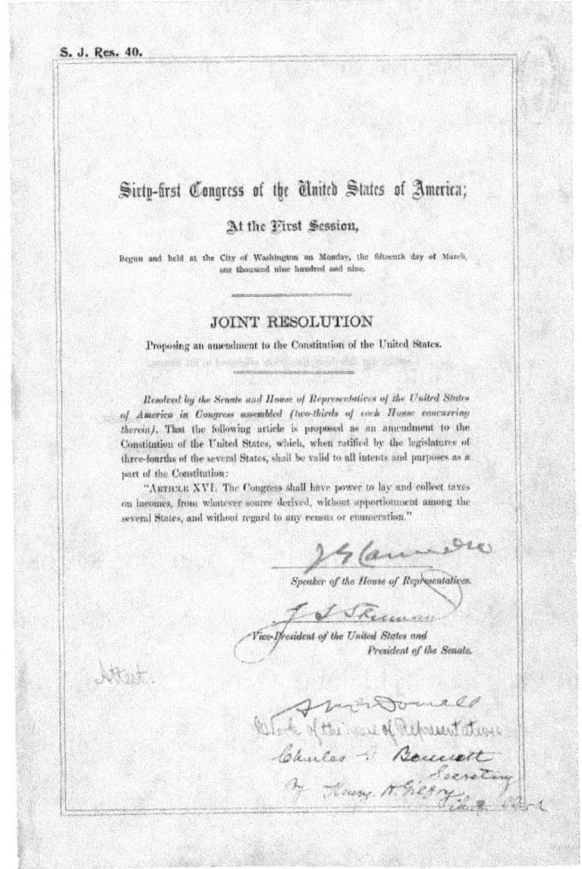

THE FAIR DEAL REPEALS SIXTEENTH

AMENDMENT!

It says: "The Congress shall have power to lay and collect taxes on incomes, from whatever source derived, without apportionment among the several States, and without regard to any census or enumeration."

The argument for an income tax was that during the Civil War, an income tax existed to finance the War. But something more direct and specific for its Repeal exists. That being the use by the Federal Reserve Board in 1910 at Jekyl Island, Georgia to insure its members that the nation would be able to service the debt they created on the nation.

This is the single most intrinsic problem with the Income tax and with it the penalties it creates on our people by fulfilling its mandate of filing tax returns and paying to them their fair share in the form of income taxes. This, THE FAIR DEAL eliminates!

As noted in the text, this Amendment could be replaced by a Balanced Budget whereby instead of balancing the budget with an income tax, the alternative to it in the form of a Fair Tax on spending.

Consequently, the States will regain control of borrowing and spending on the Federal Government because they will control its purse.

Income taxes will cease both State and Federal replaced by a tax on goods and services with some exemptions all together. Governments will shrink with opening the door once again for them to

43

be accountable to The People.

Citizen candidates, not lawyers will be elected to important positions of leadership within governmental authority. State Bars will be eliminated replaced by committees holding attorneys and judges accountable by the citizenry for unlawful and illegal rulings and orders making law from the bench.

The Chicanery caused by an unruly and out-of-control Judiciary will cease. It will be brought down by its own corruption by those it has inflicted the most pain. Society will be ruled by law; Not Those Above It!

The ruse of the sixteenth amendment will be gone because it should and the supporting cast of other statues with it. Government by design was made to serve the families of

America; not become slaves to its edicts.

Our history as a nation must return to a *Nation* of laws enforced by its Citizens upon unelected bureaucrats who use their agency to personally profit at taxpayer expense. We cannot continue to allow their conduct to impact our lives or that of our families. The time has come to act and fulfill President Kennedy's vision for America & the World!

America's destiny demands her people do for her children that which requires their economic and political security, benefit and welfare for now and generations to come.

To do that means being educated in the misconduct of this government creating a new model by which its Citizens function.

Unlike the Federal Reserve System, THE FAIR DEAL does not require an

Amendment to the Constitution to make it work. It is suggested and recommended for a Balance Budget Amendment replace it to keep the government's budget in check with its income.

Since 1913, the Federal government is dependent on tax and spend policies that cause harm to our children and families.

Inflation on prices of goods and services can be directly attributed to the number of non-backed currency dollars floating from the Federal Reserve Bank. Whether its an entry on their computers, the debt continues to grow which the cartel wants to realize the income on interest that debt generates to it.

Why this is allowed to continue should be of great concern to The People of the United States. Until this is changed and a

46

new model appears, *America* will continue to be held hostage to the bankers and their families.

In addition, the *National Debt* as a Product of the Gross National Product (GDP) is comprised of Public, Foreign Countries, and Americans. But the Federal Reserve Banks lend to the Federal government and that debt should go away. That would reduce the National Debt by 70% with the reset owed to trusts and countries.

That would greatly reduce the stress created on the taxpayers to support the debt. In effect it would relieve the burden on the people to keep more of their hard earned dollars in their pockets thereby increasing their ability to save and build an equity for themselves and their families.

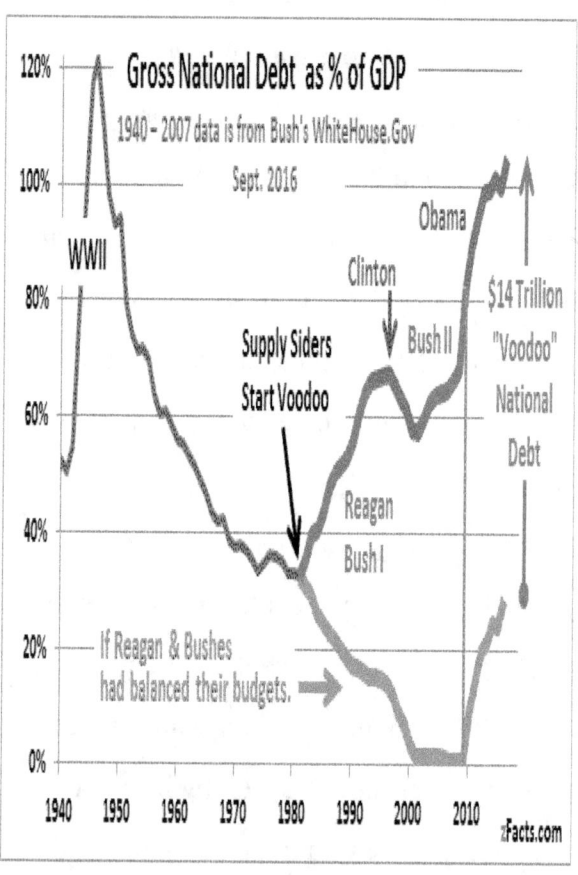

We can see from the graph how the debt is allocated and what needs to be done to rein it back. Some called it from the harm some call "Voodoo Economics" by which a cut in taxes is supposed to create a surplus by increased revenues.

A Fair Tax eliminates that problem and because revenues are based on spending and a balanced budget. That's how you keep this government solvent & its tax paying citizens able to support themselves, their families and their communities including building liquidity and equity in their bank accounts.

8. INTERNAL REVENUE [IRS]

Consistent throughout all the proceedings of events leading up to the period of the IRS were the events that caused it to be formed beginning in 1862 by President Abraham Lincoln and the Congress created & enacted the position of commissioner of Internal Revenue to tax and pay war expenses but repealed ten years later with Supreme Court ruling it unconstitutional in 1895.

So how is it that all this time has passed with America stuck in principle with an act similar to the Federal Reserve Act of 1913 and an Income Tax Amendment authorizing the government to collect income taxes on its people?

As in the case of spending & borrowing

by the federal government, there is nothing regulating it in the Constitution. It appears a Conundrum exists of legal v. illegal acts by The Congress of these United States upon The People to feather themselves at our expense.

As the chief enforcer of tax bills, the IRS over the years has grown into a leviathan engaging in practices that cause ordinary citizens to cringe by the mere utterance of their name.

In Pollock v. Farmers' Loan & Trust Co. May 21, 1895, the U.S. Supreme Court ruled the income tax a *direct* tax not *apportioned* according to the population of each state on personal income & property; 5-4 decision unconstitutional and void. It issued its ruling on the basis that the Constitution could not mandate a tax on income because *any* tax on income of the Citizens of the United States required a majority not a plurality of Congress; something still not perfected. In effect, taxation without representation was what had created the conflicts that led to War with the British at the founding of the Republic.

To some, to have it shoved down the throats of the electorate is tantamount to treason. President Kennedy knew and saw what an out-of-control government would look like and put in place "acts" to bring a plausible sustainable result to years of abuse upon the banking and finance system and ultimately the abuse upon the American taxpayer.

Because the Internal Revenue Service

is the collection agency for Congress and its budget, policies and procedures gave it broad powers over the years to investigate and prosecute acts deemed criminal by its code. THE FAIR DEAL eliminates the need for code enforcement because simply there is no tax to enforce. Government budgets must look elsewhere for its funding absent Amendments and statues to the contrary.

THE FAIR TAX on spending coupled with a Balanced Budget Amendment can satisfy the government's needs by putting to task essential services with a safety net for social needs that government has a duty to provide, preserve and protect.

National security aside, the emergence of Big government both in terms of its military and intelligence gathering apparatus causes all our citizens concern when the funding of these departments and agencies go rogue of THE PEOPLE. We as a People and America as a nation, have a duty to abuse that threatens our safety and economic security. It is is that context reforms are needed to reverse the trends that currently operate within local, State & Federal governments demanding a change that will correct years of abuse by those who have allowed it.

The Department of Revenue for the States is equipped to transition to a tax on spending for goods and services at a rate comparable to satisfy an essential budget to preserve, protect and defend threats both foreign and domestic and make policy that puts in place reforms working in the BEST

INTERESTS of the family and not its fate.

9. THE BALL DOCTRINE:
"The Rise & Fall of Modern Empires"

As though time and distance could be seen into a looking glass what is to come, history shows us what has happened to nations when the laws of economic$ are violated by those in authority.

No doubt, the nations of the World still have much to learn from the mistakes of previous generations culminating in their demise. The graph below illustrates nations' who in fact make those mistakes.

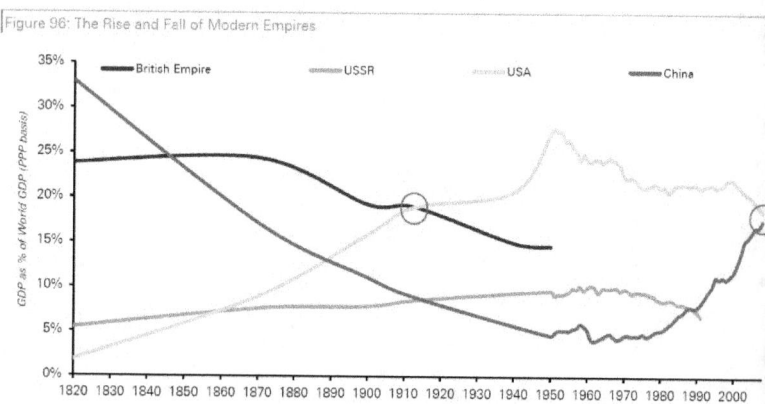

Figure 96: The Rise and Fall of Modern Empires

Source: Deutsche Bank, The World Economy, a millenial perspective (2001) Paris: OECD

It would appear to this author that for years the economic policies that created mass chaos within market conditions are based on the notion that profits trump the BEST INTERESTS of people, particularly those with the ability to exploit others for personal gain.

THE BALL DOCTRINE points out the absolute need to *reign-in* the money powers that have created so much harm to so many people throughout World History. This was President Kennedy's vision:

'He believed the family *reigned supreme* as the basic social unit of every nation'.

Speech after speech, the affirmations of America's global supremacy over those nation's who created harm to the national

57

security of the United States and its foreign policy directives were met head on by the Kennedy administration. Kennedy was a man of *destiny* and his policies created serious challenges for the establishment.

To that end, I have attempted to show what is lacking in the economic health of the nation. Central banks cause harm in the modern world because their policies are corrupted from within by policies created in 1910 and beyond starting at *Jekyl Island, Georgia.*

What is needed now is an act that corrects and cancels the harm that began over 100 years ago.

'THE BALL ACT' makes it possible. Conceived in *Liberty*, the act affirms the treason of Woodrow Wilson signing the

Federal Reserve Act on December 23, 1913 while Congress was out of session during Christmas.

A progressive, he violated his Oath of Office as President allowing enemies of The People to exploit the Constitution! As long as Central Banks could charge the federal government interest on non-backed money, the corrupt establishment allowed it to pass. President Kennedy knew the Constitutional Powers of Separation of the three branches of government and that in effect it was the United States Treasury should be in control of America's *monetary and currency policy.*

This violation of America's sovereignty showed Kennedy what previous Presidents also knew: 'The issuing of money was to come through Congress; not a Central Bank!

59

In other words, the nation's business was to stay with the nation; affirmed by previous generations and their administrations. Third party Central Banks is what Andrew Jackson shut down The Bank Of The United States during his presidency in 1833 & paid off the national debt with funds from the federal treasury backed by gold and silver bullion.

The founders had warned the nation that monetary policy could be circumvented; the nation threatened by policy violating the sovereignty of the United States causing the loss of all that had been fought and died.

With the signing of Executive Order 11110, President Kennedy effectively shut down the Federal Reserve System and they were alarmed; especially the families who benefit & support it. America's sovereignty was reaffirmed and the national debt was in check. The nation was on its way to policies that would lead to greatness amongst the World's nations affirming free-enterprise Capitalism superior to Marxist-Socialist Communism in the struggle of ideas for World dominance.

The result of this act will be to return American sovereignty back to itself with a new tax system eliminating the need for its Citizens to pay interest on debt. A balance budget insures the government stays within its means to pay for what it spends. Gold & Silver returns to back government issued Tender regulated by the States as to moneys Collected from the Fair Tax on spending.

Other debt to Trust funds & Foreign Countries paid back to refund our debt.

10. A NEW DAY!

With the advent that THE FAIR DEAL makes on the nation and the world, The People will be vilified. Years of abuse by an intrusive and corrupt system of swindle and scandal will finally be gone never to return.

The Federal Reserve System has its Tentacles in the International Monetary Fund (IMF) and the World Bank (WB).

Every nation is vulnerable to the Central Bank policy of *fiat capital* like Problems it creates in Greece & Venezula.

The Bankers have created a fail proof System of banking that works for them at expense of their depositors. By weakening the dollar through dumping dollars into the market, prices rise because it takes more of

62

it to pay for essential goods and services in relationship to the nation's Gross National Product (GNP). President Kennedy was all over it and knew that it could bankrupt the country; something he wanted to prevent!

I believe Robert Kennedy had he become President would have continued the policies his older brother created.

Both Kennedy brothers knew that War & Money corrupt a country. Both were against the exploitation of both. That is what the bankers wanted tied to The Federal Reserve System. From it, it can be conjectured that David Rockefeller and his Tri-lateral Commission & Council of Foreign Relations have directly benefited from the power the bankers have created by this debt creating system of *fiat capital.* THE FAIR DEAL!

APPENDEX

Historical Debt Outstanding - Annual 1790 - 1849

The first fiscal year for the U.S. Government started Jan. 1, 1789. Congress changed the beginning of the fiscal year from Jan. 1 to Jul. 1 in 1842, and finally from Jul. 1 to Oct. 1 in 1977 where it remains today.

Date	Dollar Amount
07/01/1849	63,061,858.69
07/01/1848	47,044,862.23
07/01/1847	38,826,534.77
07/01/1846	15,550,202.97
07/01/1845	15,925,303.01
07/01/1844	23,461,652.50
07/01/1843	32,742,922.00
01/01/1843	20,201,226.27
01/01/1842	13,594,480.73
01/01/1841	5,250,875.54
01/01/1840	3,573,343.82
01/01/1839	10,434,221.14
01/01/1838	3,308,124.07
01/01/1837	336,957.83
01/01/1836	37,513.05

01/01/1835	33,733.05
01/01/1834	4,760,082.08
01/01/1833	7,001,698.83
01/01/1832	24,322,235.18
01/01/1831	39,123,191.68
01/01/1830	48,565,406.50
01/01/1829	58,421,413.67
01/01/1828	67,475,043.87
01/01/1827	73,987,357.20
01/01/1826	81,054,059.99
01/01/1825	83,788,432.71
01/01/1824	90,269,777.77
01/01/1823	90,875,877.28
01/01/1822	93,546,676.98
01/01/1821	89,987,427.66
01/01/1820	91,015,566.15
01/01/1819	95,529,648.28
01/01/1818	103,466,633.83
01/01/1817	123,491,965.16
01/01/1816	127,334,933.74
01/01/1815	99,833,660.15
01/01/1814	81,487,846.24
01/01/1813	55,962,827.57
01/01/1812	45,209,737.90

01/01/1811	48,005,587.76
01/01/1810	53,173,217.52
01/01/1809	57,023,192.09
01/01/1808	65,196,317.97
01/01/1807	69,218,398.64
01/01/1806	75,723,270.66
01/01/1805	82,312,150.50
01/01/1804	86,427,120.88
01/01/1803	77,054,686.40
01/01/1802	80,712,632.25
01/01/1801	83,038,050.80
01/01/1800	82,976,294.35
01/01/1799	78,408,669.77
01/01/1798	79,228,529.12
01/01/1797	82,064,479.33
01/01/1796	83,762,172.07
01/01/1795	80,747,587.39
01/01/1794	78,427,404.77
01/01/1793	80,358,634.04
01/01/1792	77,227,924.66
01/01/1791	75,463,476.52
01/01/1790	71,060,508.50

President Kennedy, The Fed
And Executive Order 11110

From APFN

By Cedric X

11-20-3

Executive Order 1110 gave the US the ability to create its own money backed by silver. ...

http://www.john-f-kennedy.net/executiveorder11110.htm

On June 4, 1963, a little known attempt was made to strip the Federal Reserve Bank of its power to loan money to the government at interest. On that day President John F. Kennedy signed Executive Order No. 11110 that returned to the U.S. government the power to issue currency, without going through the Federal Reserve. Mr. Kennedy's order gave the Treasury the power "to issue silver certificates against any silver bullion, silver, or standard silver dollars in the Treasury." This meant that for every ounce of silver in the U.S. Treasury's vault, the government could introduce new money into circulation. In all, Kennedy brought nearly $4.3 billion in U.S. notes into circulation. The ramifications of this bill are enormous.

With the stroke of a pen, Mr. Kennedy was on his way to putting the Federal Reserve Bank of New York out of business. If enough of these silver certificates were to come into circulation they would have eliminated the demand for Federal Reserve notes. This is because the silver certificates are backed by silver and the Federal Reserve notes are not backed by anything. Executive Order 11110 could have prevented the national debt from reaching its current level, because it would have given the government the ability to repay its debt without going to the Federal Reserve and being charged interest in order to create the new money. Executive Order 11110 gave the U.S. the ability to create its own money backed by silver.

After Mr. Kennedy was assassinated just five months later, no more silver certificates were issued. The Final Call has learned that the Executive Order was never repealed by any U.S. President through an Executive Order and is still valid. Why then has no president utilized it? Virtually all of the nearly $6 trillion in debt has been created since 1963, and if a U.S. president had utilized Executive Order 11110 the debt would be nowhere near the current level. Perhaps the assassination of JFK was a warning to future presidents who would think to eliminate the U.S. debt by eliminating the Federal Reserve's control over the creation of money. Mr. Kennedy challenged the government of money by challenging

68

the two most successful vehicles that have ever been used to drive up debt - war and the creation of money by a privately-owned central bank. His efforts to have all troops out of Vietnam by 1965 and Executive Order 11110 would have severely cut into the profits and control of the New York banking establishment. As America's debt reaches unbearable levels and a conflict emerges in Bosnia that will further increase America's debt, one is force to ask, will President Clinton have the courage to consider utilizing Executive Order 11110 and, if so, is he willing to pay the ultimate price for doing so?

Executive Order 11110 AMENDMENT OF EXECUTIVE ORDER NO. 10289

AS AMENDED, RELATING TO THE PERFORMANCE OF CERTAIN FUNCTIONS AFFECTING THE DEPARTMENT OF THE TREASURY

By virtue of the authority vested in me by section 301 of title 3 of the United States Code, it is ordered as follows:

Section 1. Executive Order No. 10289 of September 19, 1951, as amended, is hereby further amended-

69

By adding at the end of paragraph 1 thereof the following subparagraph (j):

(j) The authority vested in the President by paragraph (b) of section 43 of the Act of May 12,1933, as amended (31 U.S.C.821(b)), to issue silver certificates against any silver bullion, silver, or standard silver dollars in the Treasury not then held for redemption of any outstanding silver certificates, to prescribe the denomination of such silver certificates, and to coin standard silver dollars and subsidiary silver currency for their redemption

and --

By revoking subparagraphs (b) and (c) of paragraph 2 thereof.

Sec. 2. The amendments made by this Order shall not affect any act done, or any right accruing or accrued or any suit or proceeding had or commenced in any civil or criminal cause prior to the date of this Order but all such liabilities shall continue and may be enforced as if said amendments had not been made.

John F. Kennedy The White House, June 4, 1963.

Of course, the fact that both JFK and Lincoln met the the same end is a mere coincidence.

Abraham Lincoln's Monetary Policy, 1865 (Page 91 of Senate document 23.)

Money is the creature of law and the creation of the original issue of money should be maintained as the exclusive monopoly of national Government.

Money possesses no value to the State other than that given to it by circulation.

Capital has its proper place and is entitled to every protection. The wages of men should be recognized in the structure of and in the social order as more important than the wages of money.

No duty is more imperative for the Government than the duty it owes the People to furnish them with a sound and uniform currency, and of regulating the circulation of the medium of exchange so that labor will be protected from a vicious currency, and commerce will be facilitated by cheap and safe exchanges.

The available supply of Gold and Silver being wholly inadequate to permit the issuance of coins of intrinsic value or paper currency convertible into coin in the volume required to serve the needs of the People, some other basis for the issue of currency must be developed, and some means other than that of convertibility into coin must be developed to prevent undue fluctuation in the value of paper currency or any other substitute for money of intrinsic value that may come into use.

The monetary needs of increasing numbers of People advancing towards higher standards of living can and should be met by the Government. Such needs can be served by the issue of National Currency and Credit through the operation of a National Banking system .The circulation of a medium of exchange issued and backed by the Government can be properly regulated and redundancy of issue avoided by withdrawing from circulation such amounts as may be necessary by Taxation, Redeposit, and otherwise. Government has the power to regulate the currency and credit of the Nation.

Government should stand behind its currency and credit and the Bank deposits of the Nation. No individual should suffer a loss of money through depreciation or inflated currency or Bank bankruptcy.

Government possessing the power to create and issue currency and creditas money and enjoying the right to withdraw both currency and credit from circulation by Taxation and otherwise need not and should not borrow capital at interest as a means of financing Governmental work and public enterprise. The Government should create, issue, and circulate all the currency and credit needed to satisfy the spending power of the Government and the buying power of the consumers. The privilege of creating and issuing money is not only the supreme prerogative of Government, but it is the Governments greatest creative opportunity.

By the adoption of these principles the long felt want for a uniform medium will be satisfied. The taxpayers will be saved immense sums of interest, discounts, and exchanges. The financing of all public enterprise, the maintenance of stable Government and ordered progress, and the conduct of the Treasury will become matters of practical administration. The people can and will be furnished with a currency as safe as their own Government. Money will cease to be master and become the servant of humanity. Democracy will rise superior to the money power.

Some information on the Federal Reserve The Federal Reserve, a Private Corporation One of the most common concerns among people who engage in any effort to reduce their taxes is, "Will keeping my money hurt the government's ability to pay it's bills?"

73

As explained in the first article in this series, the modern withholding tax does not, and wasn't designed to, pay for government services. What it does do, is pay for the privately-owned Federal Reserve System.

Black's Law Dictionary defines the "Federal Reserve System" as, "Network of twelve central banks to which most national banks belong and to which state chartered banks may belong. Membership rules require investment of stock and minimum reserves."

Privately-owned banks own the stock of the Fed. This was explained in more detail in the case of Lewis v. United States, Federal Reporter, 2nd Series, Vol. 680, Pages 1239, 1241 (1982), where the court said:

Each Federal Reserve Bank is a separate corporation owned by commercial banks in its region. The stock-holding commercial banks elect two thirds of each Bank's nine member board of directors.

Similarly, the Federal Reserve Banks, though heavily regulated, are locally controlled by their member banks. Taking another look at Black's Law Dictionary, we find that these privately owned banks actually issue money:

Federal Reserve Act. Law which created Federal Reserve banks which act as agents in maintaining money reserves, issuing money in the form of bank notes, lending money to banks, and supervising banks. Administered by Federal Reserve Board (q.v.).

The FED banks, which are privately owned, actually issue, that is, create, the money we use. In 1964 the House Committee on Banking and Currency, Subcommittee on Domestic Finance, at the second session of the 88th Congress, put out a study entitled Money Facts which contains a good description of what the FED is:

The Federal Reserve is a total money-making machine. It can issue money or checks. And it never has a problem of making its checks good because it can obtain the $5 and $10 bills necessary to cover its check simply by asking the Treasury Department's Bureau of Engraving to print them.

As we all know, anyone who has a lot of money has a lot of power. Now imagine a group of people who have the power to create money. Imagine the power these people would have. This is what the Fed is.

No man did more to expose the power of the Fed than Louis T. McFadden, who was the Chairman of the House Banking Committee back in the 1930s. Constantly pointing out that monetary issues shouldn't be partisan, he criticized both the Herbert Hoover and Franklin Roosevelt administrations. In describing the Fed, he remarked in the Congressional Record, House pages 1295 and 1296 on June 10, 1932, that:

Mr. Chairman, we have in this country one of the most corrupt institutions the world has ever known. I refer to the Federal Reserve Board and the Federal reserve banks. The Federal Reserve Board, a Government Board, has cheated the Government of the United States and he people of the United States out of enough money to pay the national debt. The depredations and the iniquities of the Federal Reserve Board and the Federal reserve banks acting together have cost this country enough money to pay the national debt several times over. This evil institution has impoverished and ruined the people of the United States; has bankrupted itself, and has practically bankrupted our Government. It has done this through the maladministration of that law by which the Federal Reserve Board, and through the corrupt practices of the moneyed vultures who control it.

Some people think the Federal reserve banks are United States Government institutions. They are not Government institutions. They are private credit monopolies which prey upon the people of the United States for the benefit of themselves and their foreign customers; foreign and domestic speculators and swindlers; and rich and predatory money lenders. In that dark crew of financial pirates there are those who would cut a man's throat to get a dollar out of his pocket; there are those who send money into States to buy votes to control our legislation; and there are those who maintain an international propaganda for the purpose of deceiving us and of wheedling us into the granting of new concessions which will permit them to cover up their past misdeeds and set again in motion their gigantic train of crime. Those 12 private credit monopolies were deceitfully and disloyally foisted upon this country by bankers who came here from Europe and who repaid us for our hospitality by undermining our American institutions.

The Fed basically works like this: The government granted its power to create money to the Fed banks. They create money, then loan it back to the government charging interest. The government levies income taxes to pay the interest on the debt. On this point, it's interesting to note that the Federal Reserve act and the sixteenth amendment, which gave congress the power to collect income taxes, were both passed in 1913. The incredible power of the Fed over the economy is universally admitted. Some people, especially in the banking and academic communities, even support it. On the other hand, there are those, both in the past and in the present, that speak out against it. One of these men was

77

President John F. Kennedy. His efforts were detailed in Jim Marrs' 1990 book, Crossfire:

Another overlooked aspect of Kennedy's attempt to reform American society involves money. Kennedy apparently reasoned that by returning to the constitution, which states that only Congress shall coin and regulate money, the soaring national debt could be reduced by not paying interest to the bankers of the Federal Reserve System, who print paper money then loan it to the government at interest. He moved in this area on June 4, 1963, by signing Executive Order 11,110 which called for the issuance of $4,292,893,815 in United States Notes through the U.S. Treasury rather than the traditional Federal Reserve System. That same day, Kennedy signed a bill changing the backing of one and two dollar bills from silver to gold, adding strength to the weakened U.S. currency.

Kennedy's comptroller of the currency, James J. Saxon, had been at odds with the powerful Federal Reserve Board for some time, encouraging broader investment and lending powers for banks that were not part of the Federal Reserve system. Saxon also had decided that non-Reserve banks could underwrite state and local general obligation bonds, again weakening the dominant Federal Reserve banks.

A number of "Kennedy bills" were indeed issued -
the author has a five dollar bill in his possession with
the heading "United States Note" - but were quickly
withdrawn after Kennedy's death. According to
information from the Library of the Comptroller of
the Currency, Executive Order 11,110 remains in
effect today, although successive administrations
beginning with that of President Lyndon Johnson
apparently have simply ignored it and instead
returned to the practice of paying interest on Federal
Reserve notes. Today we continue to use Federal
Reserve Notes, and the deficit is at an all-time high.

The point being made is that the IRS taxes you pay
aren't used for government services. It won't hurt you,
or the nation, to legally reduce or eliminate your tax
liability.

From The Final Call, Vol15, No.6, on January 17,
1996 (USA)

<http://www.apfn.org/apfn/eo11110.pdf>http://www.
apfn.org/apfn/eo11110.pdf

http://disc.server.com/discussion.cgi?disc=149495;art
icle=46736;title=APFN

JFK vs. Federal Reserve

On June 4, 1963, a virtually unknown Presidential decree, Executive Order 11110, was signed by President John Fitzgerald Kennedy with the intention to strip the Federal Reserve Bank of its power to loan money to the United States Federal Government at interest. With the stroke of a pen, President Kennedy declared that the privately owned Federal Reserve Bank would soon be out of business. This matter has been exhaustively researched by the Christian Common Law Institute through the Federal Register and Library of Congress, and the Institute has conclude that President Kennedy's Executive Order has never been repealed, amended, or superceded by any subsequent Executive Order. In simple terms, it is still valid.

When John Fitzgerald Kennedy, author of Profiles in Courage, signed this Order, it returned to the federal government, specifically to the Treasury Department, the Constitutional power to create and issue currency -- money -- without going through the privately owned Federal Reserve Bank. President Kennedy's Executive Order 11110 gave the Treasury Department the explicit authority: "to issue silver certificates against any silver bullion, silver, or standard silver dollars in the Treasury" [the full text is displayed below]. This means that for every ounce of silver in the U.S. Treasury's vault, the government could introduce new money into circulation based on the silver bullion physically held therein. As a result, more than $4 billion in United States Notes were brought into circulation in $2 and $5 denominations.

80

Although $10 and $20 United States Notes were never circulated, they were being printed by the Treasury Department when Kennedy was assassinated.

Certainly it's obvious that President Kennedy knew that the Federal Reserve Notes being circulated as "legal currency" were contrary to the Constitution of the United States, which calls for issuance of "United States Notes" as interest-free and debt-free currency backed by silver reserves in the U.S. Treasury. Comparing a "Federal Reserve Note" issued from the private central bank of the United States (i.e., the Federal Reserve Bank a/k/a Federal Reserve System), with a "United States Note" from the U.S. Treasury (as issued by President Kennedy's Executive Order), the two almost look alike, except one says "Federal Reserve Note" on the top while the other says "United States Note". In addition, the Federal Reserve Note has a green seal and serial number while the United States Note has a red seal and serial number. Following President Kennedy's assassination on November 22, 1963, the United States Notes he had issued were immediately taken out of circulation, and Federal Reserve Notes continued to serve as the "legal currency" of the nation.

Kennedy knew that if the silver-backed United States Notes were widely circulated, they would eliminated the demand for Federal Reserve Notes. This is a simple matter of economics. USNs were backed by silver and FRNs were (still are) backed by nothing of intrinsic value. As a result of Executive Order 11110, the national debt would have prevented from reaching its current level (almost all of the $9 trillion in federal debt has been created since 1963). Executive Order 11110 also granted the U.S. Government the power to repay past debt without further borrowing from the privately owned Federal Reserve which charged both principle and interest and all new "money" it "created." Finally, Executive Order 11110 gave the U.S.A. the ability to create its own money backed by silver, again giving money real value.

Perhaps President Kennedy's assassination was a warning to future presidents not to interfere with the private Federal Reserve's control over the creation of money. For, with true courage, JFK had boldly challenged the two most successful vehicles that have ever been used to drive up debt: 1) war (i.e., the Vietnam war); and, 2) the creation of money by a privately owned central bank. His efforts to have all U.S. troops out of Vietnam by 1965 combined with Executive Order 11110 would have destroyed the profits and control of the private Federal Reserve Bank.

Executive Order 11110, the AMENDMENT of EXECUTIVE ORDER No. 10289, as amended RELATING to the PERFORMANCE of CERTAIN

FUNCTIONS AFFECTING the DEPARTMENT of the TREASURY:

By virtue of the authority vested in me by section 301 of Title 3 of the United States Code, it is ordered as follows:

SECTION 1. Executive Order No. 10289 of September 19, 1951, as amended, is hereby further amended (a) By adding at the end of paragraph 1 thereof the following subparagraph (j): "(j) The authority vested in the President by paragraph (b) of section 43 of the Act of May 12, 1933, as amended (31 U.S.C. 821 (b)), to issue silver certificates against any silver bullion, silver, or standard silver dollars in the Treasury not then held for redemption of any outstanding silver certificates, to prescribe the denominations of such silver certificates, and to coin standard silver dollars and subsidiary silver currency for their redemption," and (b) By revoking subparagraphs (b) and (c) of paragraph 2 thereof.

SECTION 2. The amendment made by this Order shall not affect any act done, or any right accruing or accrued or any suit or proceeding had or commenced in any civil or criminal cause prior to the date of this Order but all such liabilities shall continue and may be enforced as if said amendments had not been made.

JOHN F. KENNEDY

THE WHITE HOUSE,

June 4, 1963

As said, Executive Order 11110 is still valid. According to Title 3, United States Code, Section 301 dated January 26, 1998: Executive Order (EO) 10289 dated Sept. 17, 1951, 16 F.R. 9499, was as amended by:

EO 10583, dated December 18, 1954, 19 F.R. 8725;

EO 10882 dated July 18, 1960, 25 F.R. 6869;

EO 11110 dated June 4, 1963, 28 F.R. 5605;

EO 11825 dated December 31, 1974, 40 F.R. 1003;

EO 12608 dated September 9, 1987, 52 F.R. 34617

The 1974 and 1987 amendments, added after Kennedy's 1963 amendment, did not change or alter any part of Kennedy's EO 11110. A search of Clinton's 1998 and 1999 EO's and Presidential Directives has shown no reference to any alterations, suspensions, or changes to EO 11110.

The Federal Reserve Bank, a.k.a Federal Reserve System, is a Private Corporation. Black's Law Dictionary defines the "Federal Reserve System" as:

"Network of twelve central banks to which most national banks belong and to which state chartered banks may belong. Membership rules require investment of stock and minimum reserves." privately owned banks own the stock of the FED. This was explained in more detail in the case of Lewis v. United States, Federal Reporter, 2nd Series, Vol. 680, Pages 1239, 1241 (1982), where the court said: "Each Federal Reserve Bank is a separate corporation owned by commercial banks in its region. The stockholding commercial banks elect two-thirds of each Bank's nine member board of directors." In short, Federal Reserve Banks are locally controlled by their member banks.

Also, according to Black's Law Dictionary, these privately owned banks are "allowed" to issue money: "The Federal Reserve Act, created Federal Reserve banks which act as agents in maintaining money reserves, issuing money in the form of bank notes, lending money to banks, and supervising banks as administered by Federal Reserve Board (q.v.)." Thus the privately owned Federal Reserve (FED) banks are allowed to actually issue (create) the "money" we use.

In 1964, the House Committee on Banking and Currency, Subcommittee on Domestic Finance, at the second session of the 88th Congress, put out a study entitled Money Facts which contains a good description of what the FED is: "The Federal Reserve is a total moneymaking machine. It can issue money or checks. And it never has a problem of making its checks good because it can obtain the $5 and $10 bills necessary to cover its check simply by asking the Treasury Department's Bureau of Engraving to print them." Any one person or any closely knit group that has a lot of money has a lot of power. Imagine a group of people with the power to create money. Imagine the power these people would have. This is exactly what the privately owned FED is!

No man did more to expose the power of the FED than Louis T. McFadden, who was the Chairman of the House Banking Committee back in the 1930s. In describing the FED, he remarked in the Congressional Record, House pages 1295 and 1296 on June 10, 1932:

Mr. Chairman, we have in this country one of the most corrupt institutions the world has ever known. I refer to the Federal Reserve Board and the Federal reserve banks. The Federal Reserve Board, a Government Board, has cheated the Government of the United States and he people of the United States out of enough money to pay the national debt. The depredations and the iniquities of the Federal Reserve Board and the Federal reserve banks acting together have cost this country enough money to pay the national debt several times over. This evil institution has impoverished and ruined the people of the United States; has bankrupted itself, and has practically bankrupted our Government. It has done this through the maladministration of that law by which the Federal Reserve Board, and through the corrupt practices of the moneyed vultures who control it.

Some people think the Federal Reserve Banks are United States Government institutions. They are not Government institutions, departments, or agencies. They are private credit monopolies, which prey upon the people of the United States for the benefit of themselves and their foreign customers. Those 12 private credit monopolies were deceitfully placed upon this country by bankers who came here from Europe and who repaid us for our hospitality by undermining our American institutions.

The FED basically works like this: The government granted its power to create money to the FED banks. They create money, then loan it back to the government charging interest. The government levies income taxes to pay the interest on the debt. On this point, it's interesting to note that the Federal Reserve Act and the sixteenth amendment, which gave congress the power to collect income taxes, were both passed in 1913. The incredible power of the FED over the economy is universally admitted. Some people, especially in the banking and academic communities, support it. On the other hand, there are those like President John F. Kennedy, that have spoken out against it. His efforts were lauded about in Jim Marrs' 1990 book Crossfire:

Another overlooked aspect of Kennedy's attempt to reform American society involves money. Kennedy apparently reasoned that by returning to the constitution, which states that only Congress shall coin and regulate money, the soaring national debt could be reduced by not paying interest to the bankers of the Federal Reserve System, who print paper money then loan it to the government at interest. He moved in this area on June 4, 1963, by signing Executive Order 11110 which called for the issuance of $4,292,893,815 in United States Notes through the U.S. Treasury rather than the traditional Federal Reserve System. That same day, Kennedy signed a bill changing the backing of one and two dollar bills from silver to gold, adding strength to the weakened U.S. currency.

Kennedy's comptroller of the currency, James J. Saxon, had been at odds with the powerful Federal Reserve Board for some time, encouraging broader investment and lending powers for banks that were not part of the Federal Reserve system. Saxon also had decided that non-Reserve banks could underwrite general obligation bonds, again weakening the dominant Federal Reserve banks."

In a speech made to Columbia University on Nov. 12, 1963, ten days before his assassination, President John Fitzgerald Kennedy said: "The high office of the

President has been used to foment a plot to destroy the American's freedom and before I leave office, I must inform the citizen of this plight." In this matter, John Fitzgerald Kennedy appears to be the subject of his own book... a true Profile of Courage. According to the Constitution of the United States, (Article 1 Section 8), only Congress has the authority to coin Money, regulate the Value thereof, and of foreign Coin, and fix the Standard of Weights and Measures. However, since 1913 this Article has been ignored by creation and existence of the Federal Reserve Act, which has given a private owned corporation the power and authority to "create" and coin the money of United States. The Federal Reserve is comprised of 12 private credit monopolies who have been given the authority to control the supply of the "Federal Reserve Notes," interest rates and all the other monetary and banking phenomena.

The way the Federal Reserve works is this: 12 private credit monopolies "create", (print), Federal Reserve Notes that are then "lent" to the American government. This is a circular affair in that the government grants the FED power to create the money, which the FED then loans back to the government, charging interests. The government levies income taxes to pay the interest on the debt. It is interesting to note that the Federal Reserve Act and the sixteenth amendment which gave congress the power to collect income taxes, were both passed in 1913. The Federal Reserve Notes are not backed by anything of "intrinsic" value. (i.e., gold or silver).

89

On June 4, 1963, President, John Fitzgerald Kennedy signed a Presidential decree, Executive Order 11110, which stripped the Federal Reserve Banking System of its power to loan money to the United States Federal Government at interest. This decree meant that for every ounce of silver in the U.S. Treasury's vault, the U.S. government could introduce new money into circulation based on the silver bullion physically held therein. As a result, more than $4 trillion in United States Notes were brought into circulation in $2 and $5 denominations. $10 and $20 United States Notes were never circulated but were being printed by the Treasury Department when Kennedy was assassinated. Kennedy knew that if the silver backed United States Notes were widely circulated, they would have eliminated the demand for Federal Reserve Notes. By giving the U.S. Treasury the Constitutional authority to coin U.S. money once again, EO 11110 would thus prevent the national debt from rising due to "usury" that the American people are charged for "borrowing" (i.e., using) FRN's.

Kennedy knew that, if Congress coined and regulated money, as the Constitution states, the national debt would be reduced by not paying interest to the 12 credit monopolies. This in itself would have allowed the American people freedom to freely use all the money they have earned, enabling the economy to grow. Now, Executive Order 11110 is still in effect, even though no U.S. President has had the courage to follow it. As Americans, it is our duty to question the Federal Reserve System and the power that we have given it by electing presidents that lack the courage of John Fitzgerald Kennedy.

More on JFK's Executive Order 11110:
http://www.rense.com/general44/exec.htm

REPRINTED BY PERMISSION

FOUNDATION FOR TRUTH & LAW 2017